English Revision

Maddy Barnes

Rising Stars UK Ltd, 7 Hatchers Mews, Bermondsey Street,
London SE1 3GS
www.risingstars-uk.com

Every effort has been made to trace copyright holders and obtain
their permission for the use of copyright materials. The publishers
will gladly receive information enabling them to rectify any error
or omission in subsequent editions. All facts are correct at time of
going to press.

First published 2013
Reprinted with revisions 2013, 2014
This edition incorporating revisions 2014

Text, design and layout © Rising Stars UK Ltd 2014
Project manager: Dawn Booth
Editorial: Marieke O'Connor
Proofreader: David Hemsley
Design: Words & Pictures Ltd, London
Cover design: Marc Burville-Riley

Acknowledgements:
p.7 *The Falcon's Malteser*, Anthony Horowitz, published by
Walker Books; p.7 illustration iStock / Mr Timmi; p.9 *China Road*,
Rob Gifford, published by Bloomsbury; p.9 *The Rough Guide to
China*, David Leffman & Simon Lewis, published by Penguin; p.10
Trash, Andy Mulligan, published by David Fickling. Reprinted by
permission of The Random House Group; p.15 *Island Man*, by Grace
Nichols, in *The Fat Black Women's Poems*, published by Virago,
an imprint of Little Brown Book Group; p.17 *Percy Jackson and
the Lightning Thief*, Rick Riordan, Penguin/Hyperion; p.19 'Four
Leopards Killed Weekly in India', Wanderlust.co.uk; p.21 *Anthem
for Doomed Youth*, Wilfred Owen, published by Random House;
p.23 'Ironic', Alanis Morisette, Universal/Sony; pp.25, 27 *Bootleg*,
Alex Shearer, published by Macmillan Children's Books, London, UK;
p.29 *Gust Becos I Cud Not Spel*, Brian Patten, Rogers, Coleridge &
White; p.30 *Stop All the Clocks* by W.H. Auden: permission granted
by Curtis Brown on behalf of the W. H. Auden Society; p.34 *Roll of
Thunder, Hear My Cry*, Mildred D. Taylor, published by Penguin.
We have been unable to trace the copyright holder of the following
poem: p.15 *The Fringe of the Sea*, L.A. Hendriks.

All rights reserved. No part of this publication may be reproduced,
stored in a retrieval system, or transmitted, in any form by any
means, electronic, mechanical, photocopying, recording or
otherwise, without prior permission of Rising Stars.

British Library Cataloguing-in-Publication Data
A CIP record for this book is available from the British Library.

ISBN: 978-1-78339-422-7

Printed in India by Multivista Global Ltd

Contents

How to use this book

What we have included:

- Those topics at Level 5 that are trickiest to get right.

- ALL Level 6 content so you know that you are covering all the topics that you need to understand in order to achieve Level 6.

- We have also put in a selection of our favourite test techniques, tips for revision and some advice on what the National Tests are all about, as well as the answers so you can see how well you are getting on.

AF5

Explaining how language is used

Skilful writers use emotive language that deliberately stirs up emotions in readers such as anger, guilt, sympathy and support. You will need to develop reading skills which help you to identify emotive language and comment on how effective it is. You don't always need to understand every word to sense the mood of a text and identify the emotions the writer wants to arouse.

Common features of emotive language

Alliteration:
closely connected words beginning with the same letter, usually a consonant, for example 'burning bushes', 'leaping lizards'.

Enjambment:
a line ending, in which the syntax, rhythm and thought are continued and completed in the next line.

Onomatopoeia:
use of words which echo their meaning in sound, for example 'snap, crackle and pop!'

Personification:
a technique of presenting things which are not human as if they were human , for example 'The lights seemed to wink at each other as the bushes smothered her steps home.'

Examples of emotive language	How this evokes sadness about the war
pallor of the girls' brows	These girls are the girlfriends and young wives from the soldiers' village.
Their flowers the tenderness of patient minds	Many soldiers were not buried but left in no-man's land. 'Patient minds' could be parents of the dead soldiers who may be unaware of the death of their son.
And each slow dusk a drawing-down of blinds	The parents of the dead soldiers would draw the blinds in respect for their sons.

20

1 Introduction – This section tells you what you need to do to get to Level 6. It picks out the key learning objective and explains it simply to you.

2 Tip boxes – These provide test hints and general tips on getting the best marks in the National Tests.

3 Practice questions – This is where you have to do the work! Try each question then check your answer.

AF5

Read this poem which was written by Wilfred Owen after his experience of being a soldier in World War I and look at the examples of emotive language given on the previous page.

Anthem for Doomed Youth

What passing-bells for these who die as cattle?
Only the monstrous anger of the guns.
Only the stuttering rifles' rapid rattle
Can patter out their hasty orisons.
No mockeries now for them; no prayers nor bells;
Nor any voice of mourning save the choirs, –
The shrill, demented choirs of wailing shells;
And bugles calling for them from sad shires.

What candles may be held to speed them all?
Not in the hands of boys but in their eyes
Shall shine the holy glimmers of goodbyes.
The pallor of girls' brows shall be their pall;
Their flowers the tenderness of patient minds,
And each slow dusk a drawing-down of blinds

by Wilfred Owen

passing-bells funeral bells

orisons prayers

mockeries ceremonies which seem meaningless now

shires counties

pallor paleness

pall funeral sheet

3

Task 1

Create two examples of alliteration and personification related to school.

_____

_____

_____

_____

_____

_____

_____

_____

_____

 TOP TIP   You will need to be able to analyse the structure of different texts and discuss them in detail. To do this effectively, you will need a strong subject knowledge of different structural features.   TOP TIP

2

21

Identifying points in a text

By Level 6, you will need to be confident at scanning and identifying the main points in texts. While reading through a variety of different texts, you will need to identify the main sentences in each paragraph.

In the Level 6 reading test, there will be some vocabulary which is difficult to understand. You will need to build on your reading for meaning skills and use a range of strategies to understand what unknown words might mean.

When you are reading a longer text you may need to identify key information or reduce the text to its most important parts. You will need to search for the information that is relevant to the question and ignore everything else. Use the wording in the question to structure your answers.

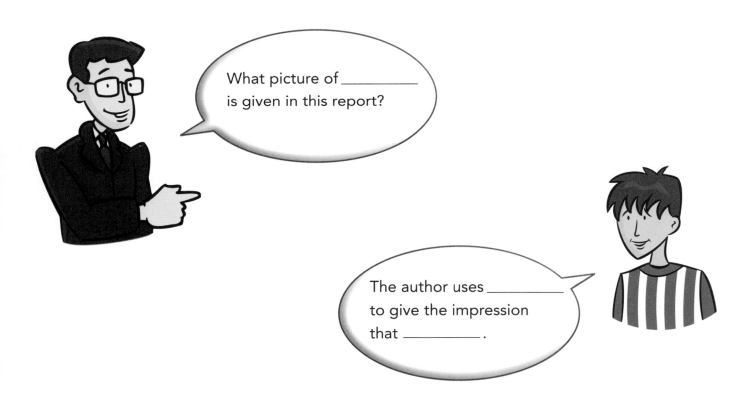

What picture of _____ is given in this report?

The author uses _____ to give the impression that _____ .

TOP TIP  **TOP TIP**

Use a dictionary or a thesaurus to increase your vocabulary. Create a bank of synonyms for yourself – this will improve the quality of your writing. For example, different words for hot include: sweltering, muggy, balmy, blistering, roasting, fiery, stifling and humid.

The Falcon's Malteser

Dear Reader,

My name is Tim Diamond, but I don't know why I'm telling you that because the one thing I don't need right now is an introduction. The last time I introduced myself, I took two bullets in the chest. It's lucky I was hiding behind the chest at the time or I could have got hurt. Getting shot at is all in a day's work for me and I'm glad I don't do overtime. The streets where I live are pretty mean. And I mean mean. And not at all pretty.

by Anthony Horowitz

Task 1

Read the above introduction to *The Falcon's Malteser*, by Anthony Horowitz. How does the writer use language to engage with the reader?

_____

_____

_____

_____

_____

Task 2

What impression does the author give you about the streets where Tim Diamond lives?

_____

_____

_____

_____

_____

Using information from different sources

The Level 6 reading test booklet usually consists of two or more different texts which are broadly related, as the context for each section covers a similar theme.

One of the skills you will need to be able to apply is to make detailed comparisons between two different sources. This could involve finding similarities (clearly stating what the texts have in common) as well as differences.

Another skill you will need to develop when using information from different sources is collating ideas to strengthen an argument or viewpoint. For example, if you were writing a report about how good a school was, you would read a range of sources in order to make sure you had a well-rounded, strong viewpoint. You might interview parents, staff and pupils to gain their opinions as well as reading any external reports about the school. After reading all of the relevant information you should be able to identify any sources which support or contradict a particular viewpoint.

Level 6 readers can recognise when writing is subjective or objective.

Subjective writing gives facts that you cannot evaluate – you have to accept it or reject it. It is usually written as somebody's opinion, feelings or thoughts.

Objective writing gives facts that you can evaluate for yourself. It usually consists of facts and figures and should not contain opinions or personal beliefs.

Some texts may combine subjective writing and objective writing. For example, a biographer may provide facts alongside an opinion. On the next page are two examples of travel writing. One is an extract from *China Road* by Rob Gifford and the other is from *The Rough Guide to China* by David Leffman and Simon Lewis. Using the definitions of subjective writing and objective writing, identify and justify which extract is subjective writing and which is objective.

TOP TIP You will need to familiarise yourself with the range of genres you may be asked to read, for example newsletters, emails, information texts, explanations, narrative, poetry, points of view, letters, brochures, postcards and play scripts. **TOP TIP**

Extract 1 *China Road*

After dinner, I wander slowly back down the Bund, avoiding the legion of beggars loitering at the door of the restaurant, heading across the road to the walkway on the waterfront where I had tried to jog earlier in the evening. You can keep Fifth Avenue, and Piccadilly, and the Champs Élysées. This is my favourite urban walk in all of the world. There is nothing quite like it, especially on a hot summer's evening. The energy, the hope, the possibilities, the past, the future, it is all here. Downtown Shanghai makes you feel that finally, after centuries of trying, China may be on the edge of greatness once again.

by Rob Gifford

Extract 2 *The Rough Guide to China*

Shanghai's original signature skyline, and the first stop for any visitor is the Bund, a strip of grand colonial edifices on the west bank of the Huangpu River, facing the skyscrapers of Pudong on the opposite shore. Since 1949, it's been known officially as Zhongshan Lu, but it's better known among locals as Wai Tan (literally 'Outside Beach'). Named after an old Anglo-Indian term, 'bunding' (the embanking of a muddy foreshore), the Bund was old Shanghai's commercial heart, with the river on one side, and the offices of the leading banks and trading houses on the other.

by David Leffman and Simon Lewis

Task 1

Using the two extracts above, identify which is subjective information and which is objective information. Record three examples of each in the table below.

Subjective	Objective

Using quotations

Throughout the Level 6 reading test, you may be asked to support your answer with quotations from the extract, or be asked to refer to a particular section of the reading booklet in your answers. These questions are testing your ability to:

(1) quickly find the information required for the answer

(2) choose at least one quotation which will support your viewpoint

(3) quote accurately from the extract by copying the word(s) or phrase exactly, and put inverted commas around the whole quotation.

Usually the question itself will indicate the length of quotation required to support your answer. If the question is phrased in this way: 'Use short quotations to support your answer,' you will be expected to find word(s) or short phrases. However, if the question is worth two or more marks, you may need to choose a longer quotation or you may need to select more than one quotation to support your answer.

TOP TIP Using quotations does not mean copying out chunks from the extract. Some questions may ask you to find and copy a particular word or phrase from the text. If the question asks you to refer to the text in your answer or support your answer with quotations, you must choose the relevant section of the text and quote, using inverted commas. **TOP TIP**

Read the extract below, 'I fell in love', from *Trash* by Andy Mulligan, and answer the questions on the next page.

Trash

I fell in love.

I fell in love with the eyes looking at me, and the smiles. I think charity work is the most seductive thing in the world, and I'd never done it before. For the first time in your life you're surrounded by people who tell you you're making a difference. The Behala children are beautiful and to see them on the rubbish tips all day can break your heart. If you come to this country, do the tourist things. But come to Behala too and see the mountains of trash, and the children who pick over them. It is a thing to change your life.

by Andy Mulligan

Task 1

After reading the extract on page 10 taken from *Trash* by Andy Mulligan, find and copy a phrase which shows how the author expresses his view of charity work.

_____

_____

_____

Task 2

Give a short quotation from the extract, which shows that the author is urging the reader to visit Behala.

_____

_____

_____

Task 3

Look at the extract again. What impressions do you get about Behala and the children who live there? Support your explanation with brief quotations.

_____

_____

_____

_____

_____

_____

_____

_____

_____

_____

Different meanings

Inference and deduction are both skills you will have demonstrated while reading at Level 5. However, a Level 6 response to these types of questions requires a deeper understanding of a range of texts. Making inferences and deductions means reading between the lines and looking beyond the obvious meaning. Identifying different layers of meaning is required at Level 6 and your response will need to be clear.

Test questions will be phrased in a range of ways. Those questions which require you to infer, and then work like a detective to solve a mystery by piecing together evidence, are often introduced by: 'What impression do you get of …?' Your answers must always be supported by evidence from the text.

Some questions may test how well you can infer information from more than one text. As you read, reflect on what information the writer is giving you as the reader. Clues are often embedded throughout different texts, some obvious and others which require the reader to piece together the jigsaw puzzle.

TOP TIP   Questions which require you to identify different layers of meaning will not explicitly state this in the question. The question will not use the words infer or deduce, but may ask you to explain or describe something.   **TOP TIP**

Tough Decisions

I've made many decisions in my life, some which were easy to make (like deciding what colour to paint the bathroom) and others more difficult. Like today.

Today was tough … tougher than I could ever have imagined. Dave was a real pal, one look from him and I usually feel ready for any challenging, gruelling battle. But today was different – we needed to take a leap of faith. Preparation involved checking our safety equipment, estimating the depth of our future and one last rehearsal of what faced us. Dave's piercing blue eyes were covered as he lowered his visor. My heart beat like a drum as inch by inch I lowered myself deeper and deeper …

Task 1

Where do you think the two characters are?

_____

_____

_____

_____

Task 2

How is the main character feeling?

_____

_____

_____

_____

Task 3

What is the purpose of the first paragraph in the extract opposite?

_____

_____

_____

_____

_____

_____

_____

The wider importance of ideas

When you read, you can make deductions about what is happening. These deductions may be about:

(**1**) characters

(**2**) plot

(**3**) setting

(**4**) ideas

(**5**) themes

(**6**) a particular point of view.

A theme is an idea which runs throughout a text. After reading a text the theme may be obvious. More demanding texts may have a variety of themes which are interwoven through the text as sub-plots and you will need to think about how and why a writer might choose to write in this way.

Poetry is also a vehicle to demonstrate different themes. Figurative language, similes, metaphors and personification are all tools poets use to convey themes and moods for the reader. Poets often contrast themes such as love and hate within a poem. Level 6 readers are expected to contrast sections of the same text as well as commenting, and contrasting two or more different texts. It is important to structure your answer clearly, ensuring that you comment on each text individually and then explore the contrasting elements.

The task on the following page has a sample answer. Read this and then attempt to write an answer in your own words on a separate piece of paper.

TOP TIP These are some of the common themes in narrative: love, hatred, jealousy, friendship, revenge, a quest, good vs. evil, sacrifice, rich / poor, bravery and loyalty. **TOP TIP**

Island Man

Morning
and island man wakes up
to the sound of blue surf
in his head
the steady breaking and wombing

wild seabirds
and fishermen pushing out to sea
the sun surfacing defiantly
from the east
of his small emerald island
he always comes back

groggily groggily
comes back to sands
of a grey metallic soar
to surge of wheels
to dull North Circular roar

muffling muffling
his crumpled pillow waves
island man heaves himself

Another London day

by Grace Nichols

The Fringe of the Sea

We do not like to awaken
Far from the fringe of the sea,
We who live upon small islands.

We like to rise up early,
Quick in the agile mornings
And walk out only little distances
To look down at the water,

to know it is swaying near to us
With songs, and tides, and endless boatways,
And undulate patterns and moods.
We want to be able to saunter beside it
slowpaced in burning sunlight,
barearmed, barefoot, bareheaded,

And to stoop down by the shallows
Sifting the random water
Between assaying fingers
Like farmers do with soil,

and to think of turquoise mackerel
turning with consummate grace,
sleek and decorous
and elegant in high blue chambers.
We want to be able to walk out into it,
To work in it, dive, swim and play in it,

to row and sail
And pilot over its sandless highways,
And to hear
Its call and murmurs wherever we may be.

All who have lives upon small islands
Want to sleep and awaken
Close to the fringes of the sea.

by L.A. Hendricks

● Task 1

What do you think is the theme of each poem? If they share the same theme, do they evoke the same mood and tone?

'Island Man' conveys the message of a Caribbean man who is homesick and wakes up dreaming of his island home. As the poem continues, the reader discovers that the sounds he actually hears are the daily sounds of another day in London. Nichols uses the term 'wombing' as personification of the breaking waves, associating them with his mother, keeping him safe.

'The Fringe of the Sea' is less personal and is written in the first person plural ('we' and 'us') and immediately evokes the feeling of team work and working together with the sea. Once again the sea is personified as a team member, contributing to the lifestyle of the island by providing food.

Although both poems discuss the sea in detail, the main themes are vastly different. 'Island Man' is a personal account of one man missing his home, whereas 'The Fringe of the Sea' is a summary of how people who live in the Caribbean islands work together.

Organisation of the text

Being able to analyse the structure and organisation of a text or extract will help you to answer questions where you have to comment on the techniques which writers use. These questions test your understanding of:

(1) paragraphs or sections

(2) connectives (how the paragraphs are organised as sections and how they link together)

(3) other cohesive devices (flashbacks, rhythm of a poem)

(4) structural features in a text.

With some questions you will need to compare and contrast how different extracts are organised. You will need to know the organisational features for a range of genres and be prepared to discuss techniques. This assessment focus may ask you to comment upon different design methods: how the organisation of the text and overall layout create effects for the reader.

 **TOP TIP** You will need to be able to analyse the structure of different texts and discuss them in detail. To do this effectively, you will need strong subject knowledge of different structural features. **TOP TIP**

Task 1

How do the structure and the organisation of the opening section of the extract on the next page engage the reader?

_____

_____

_____

_____

_____

_____

Percy Jackson and the Lightning Thief
I Accidently Vaporize my Maths Teacher

Look, I didn't want to be a half-blood.

If you're reading this because you think you might be one, my advice is: close the book right now. Believe whatever lie your mom or dad told you about your birth, and try to lead a normal life.

Being a half-blood is dangerous. It's scary. Most of the time, it gets you killed in painful, nasty ways.

If you're a normal kid, reading this because you think it's fiction, great. Read on. I envy you for being able to believe that none of this ever happened.

But if you recognise yourself in these pages – if you feel something stirring inside – stop reading immediately. You might be one of us. And once you know that, it's only a matter of time before they sense it too, and they'll come for you.

Don't say I didn't warn you.

by Rick Riordan

Task 2

'Don't say I didn't warn you.' What is the author's intention by writing this?

Task 3

Why is the repeated reference to half-bloods important in this text?

Themes and purposes

The key purposes of a text are to:

(1) explain – tell how or why something works or happened

(2) instruct – give a series of steps on how to do something

(3) persuade – present arguments and opinions to influence the reader's viewpoint

(4) inform – give facts to improve understanding

(5) entertain – provide recreation and enjoyment.

Level 6 readers should be able to identify the purpose of a text and comment on its structure, layout and use of language. More challenging texts may have a variety of purposes. For example, a persuasive letter could also explain a concept, or an informative email could offer instructions. These more complex texts may require you to identify more than one purpose, presenting a multi-layered response. All these responses can be structured using the formula PEE.

When asked the following question, use the PEE formula to structure your response.

> What is the purpose of a specific text?

P: Point – make a point by identifying the purpose (to persuade the reader, to inform, etc.).

E: Evidence – identify a feature of the genre of the text and give a quote that illustrates this.

E: Explain or expand – explain how your example illustrates a feature of the genre and how it is used.

Four Leopards Killed Weekly in India

4th October 2012

A new report reveals poachers in India are killing an average of four leopards per week and selling their parts in the country's illegal wildlife trade.

A new **WWF**-supported study carried out by the wildlife trade monitoring network, **TRAFFIC**, suggests that over 2,200 leopards have been killed in India since the year 2000.

This leaves the remaining leopard population at around 10,000 and makes it a near-threatened species – one step away from being classified as endangered.

At the report's launch, Dr Chavda of **TRAFFIC** said: 'Our objective analysis has cast new light onto the sheer scale of the illicit trade in leopard parts in India, hitherto overshadowed by the trade in another of the country's national icons, the tiger.'

Ravi Singh, CEO of **WWF** India, said: 'The leopard is among the most charismatic large animals in the world and plays an important ecological role in the forests it inhabits.

'India has both domestic and international legislation to prevent illicit trading yet continues to feed demand in key markets like Myanmar, Laos and Tibet, with Delhi being a major centre of the illegal trade.'

Pollyanna Pickering is a wildlife author and artist. She said: 'The scale of the poaching of leopards revealed in the **TRAFFIC** study saddens me greatly. I worry that I am no longer painting the living environment, but simply recording the last days of our wildlife history.'

(www.wanderlust.co.uk/magazine/news/four-leopards-killed-weekly-in-india)

Task 1

Use PEE to answer the following questions:

a) What is the purpose of using bold type for parts of the text?

_____

_____

_____

b) What is the purpose of including quotations?

_____

_____

_____

c) What is the purpose of including referencing statistics?

_____

_____

_____

Explaining how language is used

Skilful writers use emotive language that deliberately stirs up emotions in readers such as anger, guilt, sympathy and support. You will need to develop reading skills which help you to identify emotive language and comment on how effective it is. You don't always need to understand every word to sense the mood of a text and identify the emotions the writer wants to arouse.

Common features of emotive language

Alliteration:
closely connected words beginning with the same letter, usually a consonant, for example 'burning bushes', 'leaping lizards'.

Enjambment:
a line ending, in which the syntax, rhythm and thought are continued and completed in the next line.

Onomatopoeia:
use of words which echo their meaning in sound, for example 'snap, crackle and pop!'

Personification:
a technique of presenting things which are not human as if they were human, for example 'The lights seemed to wink at each other as the bushes smothered her steps home.'

Examples of emotive language used in the poem on the next page	How this evokes sadness about the war
pallor of the girls' brows	These girls are the girlfriends and young wives from the soldiers' village.
Their flowers the tenderness of patient minds	Many soldiers were not buried but left in no-man's land. 'Patient minds' could be parents of the dead soldiers who may be unaware of the death of their son.
And each slow dusk a drawing-down of blinds	The parents of the dead soldiers would draw the blinds out of respect for their sons.

Read this poem which was written by Wilfred Owen after his experience of being a soldier in World War I and look at the examples of emotive language given on the previous page.

Anthem for Doomed Youth

What passing-bells for these who die as cattle?
Only the monstrous anger of the guns.
Only the stuttering rifles' rapid rattle
Can patter out their hasty orisons.
No mockeries now for them; no prayers nor bells;
Nor any voice of mourning save the choirs, –
The shrill, demented choirs of wailing shells;
And bugles calling for them from sad shires.

What candles may be held to speed them all?
Not in the hands of boys but in their eyes
Shall shine the holy glimmers of goodbyes.
The pallor of girls' brows shall be their pall;
Their flowers the tenderness of patient minds,
And each slow dusk a drawing-down of blinds.

by Wilfred Owen

passing-bells funeral bells

orisons prayers

mockeries ceremonies which seem meaningless now

shires counties

pallor paleness

pall funeral sheet

Task 1

Create two examples of alliteration and personification related to school.

_____

_____

_____

_____

_____

_____

_____

_____

 **TOP TIP** You will need to be able to analyse the structure of different texts and discuss them in detail. To do this effectively, you will need a strong subject knowledge of different structural features. **TOP TIP**

Language choice and effectiveness

Writers use language and literary features to create images to help readers understand what the writer is saying. When analysing passages, you will be expected to recognise some of these features and comment on why the author chose to use them and how effective they are.

Useful terms when analysing a text

Pathetic fallacy: where something non-human represents a human emotion (Shakespeare often uses stormy weather when a character is in turmoil).

Transferred epithets: where a descriptive word is transferred from a human to non-human object (a sleepless night, cheerful money, suicidal sky).

Sarcasm: where what is written or said is the complete opposite of what is really meant ('Are you stuck in the mud?' 'No, no, of course not, I'm just having a mud bath!').

Irony: where what is happening is the opposite of what is intended or being presented.

Paradox: a statement that appears contradictory but may actually be true.

Reverse psychology: a technique using pessimism to get a positive outcome (convincing somebody that they will not succeed, in the hope that they will).

Juxtaposition: where two or more objects, themes, characters are contrasted side by side or together.

Pathos: evoking a feeling of pity or compassion through description.

Irony, sarcasm and satire are usually used to mock somebody or something. Irony is used when there is a contradiction between an action or expression and its context.

Irony can be used as a device to develop character, plot and setting or as a tool in non-fiction, perhaps when reporting or persuading. An example of irony is saying, 'Beautiful weather we are having', when it is pouring with rain.

There are two main kinds of irony:

- situational irony is when something happens that seems especially unfair – like winning the lottery and dying the next day.

- verbal irony is saying one thing but really meaning something different.

> Ironic
>
> An old man turned ninety-eight
> He won the lottery and died the next day
> It's a black fly in your Chardonnay
> It's a death row pardon two minutes too late
> And isn't it ironic ... don't you think
>
> It's like rain on your wedding day
> It's a free ride when you've already paid
> It's the good advice that you just didn't take
> Who would've thought ... it figures
>
> A traffic jam when you're already late
> A no-smoking sign on your cigarette break
> It's like ten thousand spoons when all you need is a knife
>
> It's meeting the man of my dreams
> And then meeting his beautiful wife
> And isn't it ironic ... don't you think
> A little too ironic ... and, yeah, I really do think ...
>
> by Alanis Morissette

This extract is taken from a song called 'Ironic' by Alanis Morissette.

Task 1

Find three examples of situational irony in the extract above.

_____

_____

_____

TOP TIP   It is often easier to give an example of irony than to explain it. Irony is implied and the reader must infer (read between the lines).   **TOP TIP**

The effect of sentence structure

As a Level 6 reader, you need to recognise different sentence types as well as understand when to use them in your own writing.

Sentence type	Simple	Compound	Complex
Structure	one independent clause (can have a compound subject and verb)	two or more independent clauses joined with a semi-colon or a co-ordinating conjunction	one independent clause and one dependent clause joined by a subordinating conjunction
When used	for clarity, to convey urgency, shock or surprise, to increase the pace, to emphasise an idea	to link ideas, to add extra information, to help the writing flow fluently	to develop ideas, to add extra information or extra layers of meaning, to add variety or contrast
Example	'I wanted to play out.'	'I wanted to play out but it was raining.'	'Although it rains a lot when I want to play out, it doesn't bother me forever.'

Authors use different types of sentence structures to create different effects. As a Level 6 reader you need to understand how selected words, phrases and sentence structures affect the rest of the text and the impact they have on the reader.

The extract on the following page is taken from a novel called *Bootleg* by Alex Shearer. The Good For You Party is running the country, and forcing everyone to lead healthier lives. Chocolate and any other food containing sugar has been banned. Here a bootlegger, Smudger, is trying to convince his friend Leroy to give him some cocoa in order to make chocolate.

A series of questions is used to portray Smudger's desperation.

Using a compound sentence to link Leroy's actions.

Repeating three words ('possibly, maybe, perhaps') throughout the extract.

Using one-word-sentence answers.

Complex sentence which develops Smudger's question to Leroy.

Bootleg

'So your dad wouldn't have any in his warehouse, then? Like some left over? That nobody found? As the detectors don't work on ingredients? Possibly, maybe, perhaps?'

Leroy aimed the basketball at the hoop but missed.

'Hmm,' he said non-committally. 'Possibly, maybe, perhaps.'

'In fact,' Smudger said, warming to his theme, 'maybe you even stashed a little bit away, Leroy, that your dad doesn't know about.'

'Hmm, possibly,' Leroy admitted, taking another shot at the hoop. 'Maybe. Perhaps.'

'Only what use are ingredients, Leroy,' Smudger pointed out, 'if you don't have the inside information on how to turn them into the finished product? True?'

'Possibly, 'Leroy conceded, missing the hoop yet again. 'Maybe. Perhaps.'

by Alex Shearer

Task 1

What is the purpose of repeating three words ('possibly, maybe, perhaps') throughout the text?

_____

_____

Task 2

What is the function of Leroy using one-word answers at the end of the extract?

_____

_____

Writers' techniques

The author's viewpoint shows the writer's opinion and what he or she thinks about the topic. At Level 6, you will need to use evidence from the text to deduce the author's viewpoint.

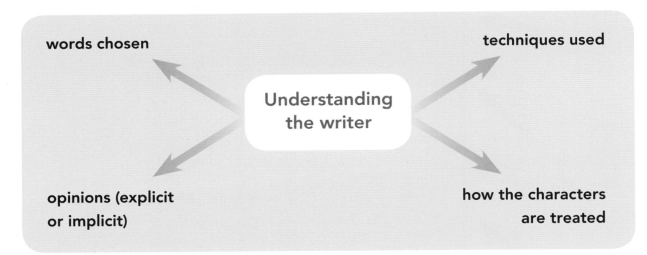

words chosen

techniques used

Understanding the writer

opinions (explicit or implicit)

how the characters are treated

Level 6 readers understand that the writer is the director and the characters are his or her creation. Everything about the characters has been decided by the writer, from their appearance and behaviour to how they sound – and even how they think! The characters are the puppets which the writer (as puppeteer) so carefully carves and controls. Through the creation of characters, you can gain an insight into the writer's mind and viewpoint.

Task 1

Writers entertain readers in a variety of ways. Sometimes they betray readers by making a character behave in a way they would not normally behave. Write four other ways that writers entertain us.

_____

_____

_____

_____

Some writers use dialogue effectively to reveal characters, and relationships between characters. Dialogue can bring a scene alive and can be a very effective way to understand the more implicit (not obvious) aspects of characters such as what they are thinking and feeling.

In another extract from *Bootleg* by Alex Shearer, the character Huntly is uncertain as to whether he is allowed honey on his sandwich, since he is living at a time when chocolate and all sugar is banned.

Bootleg

'Come on Huntly,' his mother said. 'It's not that bad, is it? What are they going to do? Come round and inspect your lunch box?'

Yes. He was being ridiculous.

'OK, honey roll, then. Thanks.'

And yet Huntly felt uneasy.

What would you have done, Dad?

But the voice in his head was silent. Maybe he would have to deal with this alone. What was happening now was something his father had never experienced. Who did know about things like the Good For You Party?

But finally the voice came, as it always did. He knew his dad wouldn't let him down.

'You be careful now, Huntly. That's all I can say. And look out for Mum too.'

'Yes, Dad,' he whispered, 'I will.'

'Sorry, Huntly, did you say something?' His mother looked up from the roll she was spreading.

'Nothing, Mum.'

by Alex Shearer

In this short extract, we learn that Huntly's father is dead. At times when he is feeling frightened and unsure, he talks to his father in his head and imagines the response. From this, we can deduce the writer's sensitivity towards Huntly. The writer wants us to know that Huntly is a 'good guy', a character who wants to do the right thing but is torn between the Good For You Party and what he knows is the right thing to do.

Commenting on a writer's viewpoint

Questions which ask the reader to comment on a writer's use of language and on what effects a text can have on a reader often begin with:

(1) How does the writer show he admires / is sympathetic / disapproves of …?

(2) How does the writer try to help the reader understand …?

(3) Why did the writer include …?

There are certain phrases which you can use to respond to AF6 questions.

By referring to …
By using the phrase …
By mentioning how …
In the first paragraph … . However, in the second paragraph … .

He looked around and it was quiet … too quiet. Tap tap. A hand on his back.

Task 1

Complete the sentence about the extract on the left. The writer makes the reader feel _____ by _____ .

Would you like to get a Level 6 in English? If so, this is the book for you, crammed full with exercises to stretch your capable mind and tease out new learning on every page! Purchase me today and you will already be on the path to success …

Task 2

Comment on the use and effect of language used in the extract on the left.

_____

_____

_____

TOP TIP  The author can appeal to the reader in many ways:
• by challenging assumptions • by addressing the reader directly
• by giving the reader a command • by shocking the reader. **TOP TIP**

Understanding a writer's point of view

Gust Becos I Cud Not Spel

Gust becos I cud not spel
It did not mean I was daft
When the boys in school red my
  riting
Some of them laffed

But now I am the dictater
They have to rite like me
Utherwise they cannot pas
Ther GCSE

Some of the girls were ok
But those who laffed a lot
Have al bean rownded up
And hav recintly bean shot

The teecher who corrected my
  speling
As not been shot at al
But four the last fifteen howers
As bean standing up against a wal

He has to stand ther until he can
  spel
Figgymisgrugifooniyn the rite way
I think he will stand ther for ever
I just inventid it today

by Brian Patten

Read Brian Patten's poem on the left and consider the following questions.

Task 1

a) What evidence is there that the boy wasn't daft?

_____

_____

_____

_____

b) What punishment does his teacher get?

_____

_____

_____

_____

Task 2

What point was Brian Patten trying to prove?

_____

_____

_____

Creating effects

All texts have the potential to have an effect on the reader. The writer can evoke strong, powerful feelings in the reader such as love, hate and jealousy. Writers make conscious decisions about the use of imagery, words, punctuation, paragraphs and layout (such as stanzas in poems) when creating the effect they want to achieve through their writing.

This version of W.H. Auden's poem was published in 1938 and is well known as a poem which evokes strong emotions from start to finish.

Stop All the Clocks

Stop all the clocks, cut off the telephone,
Prevent the dog from barking with a juicy
    bone,
Silence the pianos and with muffled drum
Bring out the coffin, let the mourners come.

Let aeroplanes circle moaning overhead
Scribbling on the sky the message He Is
    Dead,
Put crepe bows round the white necks of
    the public doves,
Let the traffic policemen wear black cotton
    gloves.

He was my North, my South, my East and
    West,
My working week and my Sunday rest,
My noon, my midnight, my talk, my song;
I thought that love would last for ever: I
    was wrong.

The stars are not wanted now: put out
    every one;
Pack up the moon and dismantle the sun;
Pour away the ocean and sweep up the
    wood.
For nothing now can ever come to any
    good.

by W.H. Auden

First stanza: A sense of denial because the writer does not want to accept the truth but instead wants to 'stop the clocks'.

Second stanza: The opening line 'Let aeroplanes circle moaning overhead,' uses moaning, a very onomatopoeic word. You can almost visualise the sound. It could also reflect the sound of the mourners in the church.

Third stanza: In this stanza the writer permits himself to remember his love. The imagery illustrates the magnitude of this love, all the compass directions and every time of day.

Fourth stanza: The atmosphere of the poem changes as the poet drifts into depression or even anger. Auden orders that nature should be discarded in his anger.

Language and the effect of time

Language is constantly evolving, which means that word meanings can change over time and some words have even become obsolete (fallen out of use or been replaced by new words). When faced with words from different eras, which have a different meaning to modern readers, we need to use the context to deduce the meaning of unfamiliar words.

An example of this is the word safe.

'Claire is safe,' shouted James to Ed.

Some readers might understand that Claire was safe as in protected and unharmed. However, more modern readers may understand safe to mean cool, good or nice.

Another example is the word sick.

'Ellie is sick,' said Luke to John.

Modern readers might interpret sick to mean cool and hip, whereas more traditional readers would understand it to mean that Ellie was actually feeling physically sick.

Task 1

Complete the table by writing in the modern definition.

Example	Traditional definition	Modern definition
cool	temperature, poise, relaxed	good, trendy, stylish
hot	temperature	
tight	where something doesn't fit into a space	
burn	when something which is hot burns you	
sweet	a sugary taste	

Task 2

Explain how the word 'wicked' could be misunderstood by modern readers: 'Osian is wicked,' shouted Anthony.

_____

_____

Texts from different times and places

You may be asked questions that:

(1) require you to call upon your knowledge of traditional stories to link ideas between texts

(2) encourage you to link popular culture and stereotypes to characters and themes in your reading

(3) require you to use your knowledge of history and 'outdated' beliefs and attitudes to comment on texts

(4) encourage you to apply your knowledge and understanding of life.

These questions usually involve a comparison between two or more extracts or a summary explaining how two or more texts are linked.

Here are some answer stems which will help you when you are comparing and contrasting two poems:

Compare	Contrast
Both poems … Similarly … In the same way … Likewise … Equally … The poems / texts agree about …	In a different way … The poems vary in … In contrast … In a different way … The texts hold opposing views on … However / Whereas …

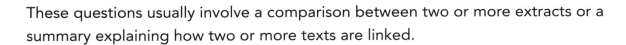

Task 1

Tick two features which all traditional tales have:

- All have a wolf
- There is a male hero
- There is a female heroine
- Animals can talk
- Good overcomes bad
- All have a death
- A character learns a lesson

Task 2

Many nursery rhymes are innocent stories but some contain morals and others even have sinister and political meanings. Use the Internet to find the origins or speculated origins for these nursery rhymes:

a) 'Sing a Song of Sixpence'_____

_____

_____

_____

b) 'Mary Had a Little Lamb'_____

_____

_____

_____

c) 'London Bridge is Falling Down'_____

_____

_____

_____

d) 'Ring a Ring o' Roses'_____

_____

_____

_____

Task 3

Look at the two poems on page 15 – 'Island Man' and 'The Fringe of the Sea'. How are the two poems similar?

_____

_____

_____

_____

_____

_____

Cultural and spiritual influences

A Level 6 reader recognises that different people have different beliefs, customs and values. You should also understand that some words have different meanings in different countries and languages.

When faced with an extract which is written from, or about, a different culture there will be some obvious clues. These could include explanations of different lifestyles or customs, different attitudes to events or situations, unfamiliar vocabulary and speech in Non-Standard English.

Read the following extract which is taken from a book called *Roll of Thunder, Hear My Cry* by Mildred D. Taylor.

Roll of Thunder, Hear My Cry

They come down like ghosts that Christmas of seventy-six. Them was hard times like now and my family was living in a shantytown right outside Shreveport. Reconstruction was just 'bout over then, and them Northern soldiers was tired of being in the South and they didn't hardly care 'bout no black folks in shantytown. And them Southern whites, they was tired of the Northern soldiers and free Negroes, and they was trying to turn things back round to how they used to be. And the colored folks … well, we was just tired. Warn't hardly no work, and during them years I s'pose it was jus' 'bout as hard being free as it was being a slave. That night they come. I can remember just as good, it was cold, so cold we had to huddle.

by Mildred D. Taylor

Task 1

The above extract is not set in modern-day England. Using the text to support your answer, explain how you know this.

_____

_____

_____

_____

Introduction to writing

Your teacher may assess your writing using these Assessment Foci (AFs):

Teacher	Pupil
AF1: Write imaginative, interesting and thoughtful texts.	AF1: My writing is imaginative, interesting and thoughtful.
AF2: Produce texts which are appropriate to task, reader and purpose.	AF2: I am able to write for different purposes and audiences according to the task set.
AF3: Organise and present whole texts effectively, sequencing and structuring information, ideas and events.	AF3: I can plan my writing and produce texts that sequence ideas, information and events within an appropriate structure.
AF4: Construct paragraphs and use cohesion within and between paragraphs.	AF4: I can use topic sentences and linking sentences to guide my reader through the text.

Assessment Foci can be grouped into three strands:

Sentence structure and punctuation	Text structure and organisation	Appropriacy and vocabulary
AF 5 and 6	**AF 3 and 4**	**AF 1 and 2**
• Variety of sentence type and length. • Range of verb forms used and shifts are managed well. • Secure range of appropriate punctuation used for clarity.	• Coherence: structure is controlled and suited to the purpose. • Cohesion: sections / paragraphs are linked to signal direction clearly for the reader. Ideas are well organised within sections / paragraphs and cohesive devices support purpose.	• Writing is adapted, addressing the target audience and is focused on the purpose, containing features of the chosen form. • Vocabulary choices are ambitious, precise, appropriate and purposeful.

● Task 1

Reflect on your own recent writing and, referring to the Assessment Foci, identify your strengths and areas for development, and list them below.

_____

_____

_____

Informal and formal language

Formal and informal styles must be chosen to suit the purpose of the writing. As a Level 6 writer, you need to identify the purpose and audience of a piece of writing. In turn, you will need to decide what form and level of formality are required.

 formality

What a day!

Your best friend has been off school today and everything has gone wrong. You want to tell your friend what has happened and decide to email her / him immediately.

 form audience purpose

Writing an email to your best friend to tell them about your day is an informal piece of writing.

Informal writing uses:
- apostrophes for contraction
- an awareness of emotions
- exclamation marks
- a chatty style (colloquialisms, slang and informal language).

However, **all** pieces of writing must be well organised, contain a range of sentence types and be supported by punctuation for clarity and meaning.

More formal pieces of writing, such as writing to the bank manager, a police report, an application for a job, a letter to the council or letters of complaint, require more formal language and different writing conventions.

Formal writing features:
- complex and passive voice sentences
- third person
- points that are clearly stated and explained without undue emotion
- punctuation is functional
- words that are written in full.

Task 1

Write the opening and closing of an informal email and a formal letter.

_____

_____

_____

Imaginative vocabulary and language

Level 6 writers are usually 'well read', meaning that they have a large vocabulary at their fingertips to use in their own writing. In order to write thoughtful, imaginative and interesting pieces, you need to continue to discover and learn new words.

Selecting vocabulary which engages, entertains and informs the reader is a skill that you will need to build upon. Understanding and creating banks of synonyms and antonyms will help you to acquire new vocabulary.

Synonym: a word with the same meaning as another.

Antonym: a word meaning the opposite of another.

● Task 1

Complete the following table.

Word	Synonyms	Antonym
nice	amiable, pleasant	nasty
dark	dusky, shadowy	
fast	rapid, brisk	
hot	scorching, sultry	
beautiful	stunning, exquisite	
loud	blaring, piercing	
sad	forlorn, sombre	
small	miniature, pocket-sized	

● Task 2

How many different words can you think of to explain the following colours? Write them in the table.

Blue	Red	Yellow
navy turquoise cobalt cyan aqua ultramarine		

TOP TIP   **TOP TIP**

To improve your use of language you could:
• select some vocabulary which is descriptive or specific to the task
• use vocabulary to interest, surprise and influence your reader
• use formal vocabulary to contribute to objective writing.

Parts of speech

Level 6 readers are expected to recognise different parts of speech within a context and discuss the purpose of word choice. Here is a brief reminder of some parts of speech:

Determiners and quantifiers

These are types of word that refer to a noun and determine which object, person or other entity the noun represents. Types of determiners include articles (a, an, the) and quantifiers (a few, a little, many, most, some). Other determiners are possessives (my, her, your, their) and demonstratives (this, that, these, those).

⬤ Task 1

Choose the right determiners from the list to complete the sentences.

a   an   some   the

a) My mum needed to buy ___ umbrella. We decided to catch ___ bus and do ____ shopping at the same time. It wasn't such ___ bad day after all.

b) The toddler dressed up like ___ Eskimo and wanted to build _____ igloo. He tried to convince ____ of his friends to join in with _____ activity.

Adverbs

These are words which modify verbs and make your writing more exciting, for example slowly. However, sometimes a more precise and carefully chosen verb is better than using a verb + an adverb. For example:

the men walked slowly → the men strolled

The positioning of adverbs in sentences can create different shades of meaning. Adverbs can be positioned before the action, after the action or at the start of the sentence.

⬤ Task 2

Read the verb + adverb and choose a more precise verb that means the same.

a) The children spoke loudly.   _____

b) The boys ran quickly.   _____

A question tag

This is a phrase added to the main part of the sentence, inviting the listener to confirm or give an opinion about the speaker's comment. For example:

> It isn't very warm today, **is it**?
>
> You have already seen this film, **haven't you**?
>
> He will come today, **won't he**?
>
> You go to school, **don't you**?

> You may be asked to:
>
> • circle the question tag in a question
>
> • add a question tag to complete a question
>
> • match some questions with appropriate question tags.

Task 3

Add a question tag to complete the following questions.

a) You have got the keys, _____

b) I will have to bake a cake now, _____

c) She could have bought a present, _____

Double negatives

Double negatives are not Standard English.

> You don't know nothing → You don't know anything / You know nothing.
>
> I ain't got none → I haven't got any.

The use of double negatives is not considered proper or Standard English.

There may be some occasions, usually when speaking, when the use of double negatives is accepted.

Nouns

Think about the words you are going to use in your writing. To improve the standard of your writing you will need to choose precise nouns for interest and clarity. Nouns are the names given to people, places, animals or things. However, nouns can be divided into further classes such as proper nouns, common nouns, collective nouns and abstract nouns.

Proper nouns

Definition: Proper nouns are names of specific people, places, times, occasions and events. For example:

Claire and **James** went to **Poland** to get married.

> **You may be asked to complete sentences like these with proper nouns:**
>
> • ___ decided to celebrate her 12th birthday with her friends.
>
> • Faye and her family went on holiday to ___ for half term.
>
> • My date of birth is the 19th ___ 2002.

TOP TIP Proper nouns are always written with a capital letter; for example, Eleanor. **TOP TIP**
Proper nouns do not usually allow a plural.

Common nouns

Definition: Common nouns name things that there are many of – animals, flowers, modes of transport, clothes, etc.

> **You may be asked to underline the common nouns in a passage like this one:**
>
> Professor Strudwick collected her items together for the lecture. All were present and correct: books, stationery, technology gadgets and, of course, her personal selection of herbal teas.

 Common nouns are not written with a capital letter.
They are usually used with a determiner: the dogs, some sweets.

Collective nouns

Definition: Collective nouns are names given to groups of people, animals or other collections.

> A litter of cubs, a pack of dogs, a squabble of seagulls, a clew of worms, a bed of cockles, a school of cod, a shoal of mackerels, a quiver of cobras, a crowd of onlookers, a choir of singers, a staff of employees, a fleet of cars, a ream of paper, a pod of peas!

Abstract nouns

Definition: Abstract nouns are names given for things that you can think about, but cannot see, hear, touch or taste, for example happiness, love, fear, bravery, courage, loyalty, patience, freedom, wisdom.

● Task 1

Draw a table like this and keep a record of any interesting nouns you could use in your writing.

Proper nouns	Common nouns	Collective nouns	Abstract nouns

TOP TIP   It is very important to use different types of nouns in your sentences and also you will need to use expanded noun phrases (e.g. the large black dog), adjectives and other figurative language to make your writing interesting for the reader.   **TOP TIP**

Connectives and cohesion

Level 6 writers use a variety of simple and complex sentences as well as a range of grammatical structures to vary length and focus. You should organise your writing so that paragraphs or sections are linked in a variety of ways to give the reader overall direction. Within paragraphs, your ideas should be organised and developed using a range of cohesive devices, such as connectives.

Connectives link together ideas in one sentence or between different sentences and paragraphs. Linking ideas and sentences gives your writing cohesion – it holds it together and gives it more meaning.

Connectives can be grouped into different types, according to their function in the sentence. Look at the types and the example given for each:

Comparison	Contrasting	Rephrasing	Emphasising	Summing up
likewise similarly equally	however although whereas	in other words	mainly mostly unfortunately	overall to conclude in summary
Listing points	**Concessions**	**Giving examples**	**Cause and effect**	**Change of topic**
to begin with in addition firstly	despite the fact nevertheless	for instance such as	therefore so because	concerning moving on to

The connectives in the table above are just an example of each category – there are many more which you may prefer to use. As a Level 6 writer, your writing should be fluent and connectives should be used accurately to support your text structure and organisation. Ensure that you use connectives which you understand, rather than using one incorrectly.

Task 1

Write a short paragraph instructing a person how to get a Level 6 in writing, using *to begin with*, *such as*, *overall* and *however* (in any order).

_____

_____

_____

TOP TIP

What is the difference between a connective and a conjunction?
Connectives are words or phrases that link ideas together.
Connectives can also be conjunctions.
Conjunctions have the job of joining two ideas in a sentence whereas other connectives join the ideas in one sentence to the ideas in another sentence or paragraph.

TOP TIP

Identifying phrases

Phrases are structural elements which may contain only one word or many words. Level 6 writers can recognise a range of phrases such as noun phrases, verb phrases, adverbial phrases, prepositional phrases and adjectival phrases.

What is a noun phrase?

Noun phrases have a noun as their key word:

> My father,
>
> Wendy,

In noun phrases where the key word is a noun, there are many ways in which you can put words in front or after the noun to expand the noun phrase:

> cat
>
> the cat
>
> the Siamese cat
>
> the black Siamese cat
>
> the old, black Siamese cat
>
> the old, black Siamese cat in the corner

These are all noun phrases.

 **TOP TIP** Pronouns can take the place of nouns so it is also possible for noun phrases to have pronouns as their key words: he instead of my father and she instead of Wendy. **TOP TIP**

What is a verb phrase?

1 A simple verb phrase consists of just a single verb:

> sing, ate, walk, said

2 It is also possible to add other words to the verb – these are called auxiliary verbs and the three most common are do, be and have:

> They **will be singing** in the final.

3 There are three verb phrases in this sentence:

> Claire **has drawn** many pictures for us. She **told** us that her teacher **had taught** her some new techniques.

What is an adjectival phrase?

An adjectival phrase is a group of words in a sentence with one or more adjectives which describe the noun:

> distinctive blue spots

What is an adverbial phrase?

An adverbial phrase is a group of words which give you more information about the time, the place or the manner of the action that is described:

> I arranged to meet him **outside the bank**.
> I waited for **an hour**, but he did not turn up.
> Creatures of all shapes and sizes are **found around the world**.

What is a prepositional phrase?

Prepositional phrases begin with a preposition followed by a word or words to complete the phrase. You can structure a prepositional phrase in three ways:

1 with a preposition followed by a noun phrase:
in the garden, to the cinema

2 with a preposition followed by an adverb:
over there, in here

3 with a preposition followed by an adjective:
at best

TOP TIP

You will need to identify the subject and object in a sentence. Some questions may ask you to identify the subject noun phrase (SNP) or the object noun phrase (ONP).

The subject noun is the noun doing the action (governs the main verb) and the object noun is the noun having the action done to it (affected by the main verb).

My younger sister Claire will be modelling in the fashion show.

↓ subject noun phrase   ↓ object noun phrase

TOP TIP

● Task 1

Label the subject noun phrase SNP and the object noun phrase ONP.

a) The ninety-year-old man stumbled up the crooked path.

b) The top goalscorer won the golden boot award.

Using prepositional phrases accurately

A prepositional phrase has two basic parts: a preposition plus a noun or a pronoun that serves as the object of the preposition. A preposition is a word that shows *how* a noun or a pronoun is related to another word in a sentence. Here are some of the most common prepositions.

about	behind	except	outside
above	below	for	past
across	beneath	near	through
after	between	of	until
against	by	off	with
before	during	on	without

Sentences without prepositional phrases can be vague and ambiguous. For example:

We do not know who the children are, what they won or how they celebrated.

The children have won a variety and have celebrated.

Since prepositional phrases act as an adjective or an adverb, we can answer some of these queries by adding prepositional phrases. As an adjective, the prepositional phrase will answer which one? As an adverb, the prepositional phrase will answer questions such as how, when and where? Once we add these details the sentence is much easier to understand:

> For many years the children from Greenchester Primary School have won a variety of sporting and debating competitions and have celebrated with parties and assemblies.

Prepositional phrases answer questions for the reader by adding details and explaining where, when, which and how.

 **Task 2**

Add prepositional phrases to create a more detailed description to the following:

The teenagers have dressed up and danced.

_____

_____

_____

Identifying independent and dependent clauses

Independent clauses have a subject + verb and could stand alone as a sentence:

> the boy looked nervous

Dependent clauses (subordinate clauses) have a subject + verb and start with a subordinate conjunction:

> because it was late
> until she was ready
> if she had time
> whenever he could

How do you combine independent and dependent clauses?

1 Whenever he had time, he went to the gym.
Dependent clause first: needs a comma before the independent clause.

2 He went to the gym whenever he had time.
Independent clause first: does not need a comma before the dependent clause.

3 He went, whenever he had time, to the gym.
Dependent clause in the middle of a sentence: needs a comma before and after it.

Task 1

Using the guidance above on how to combine independent and dependent clauses, rewrite each sentence below in two alternative ways.

a) Because she was tired, she went to bed early.

_____

_____

b) He tried, whenever he could, to do his best in school.

_____

_____

Tenses and modal verbs

Verb tenses are tools you use to express time.

Here is a verb tense overview:

Simple present	Simple past	Simple future
I write in my diary every day.	Yesterday I wrote in my diary.	Tomorrow I am going to write in my diary.
Present continuous	**Past continuous**	**Future continuous**
I am writing in my diary now.	I was writing my diary last night when you rang.	I will be writing my diary after dinner.
Present perfect	**Past perfect**	**Future perfect**
I have written in my diary.	I had written in my diary before school.	I will have written in my diary before I see you.
Present perfect continuous	**Past perfect continuous**	**Future perfect continuous**
I have been writing in my diary for five years.	I had been writing in my diary for a long time before I bought a new one.	I will have been writing in my diary for an hour by the time you get here.

As a Level 6 writer, it is important that you use tenses accurately in your own writing. You may also be asked to rewrite sentences in different tenses. In order to complete tense exercises accurately, you will need to understand both regular and irregular verb forms.

Modal verbs

The main modal verbs are *will*, *would*, *can*, *could*, *may*, *might*, *shall*, *should*, *must* and *ought*. Modal verbs are important for expressing degrees of certainty.

I **might** go swimming later on with my friends.

You **should** know how to do that.

We **mustn't** run in the corridors at school.

 **TOP TIP** Past participles are also used to make one of the past forms for the modal verbs (modal auxiliaries). These forms use modal + have + the past participle. Here are some examples:
• could have gone • may have been • should have known
• might have seen • would have written • must have forgotten **TOP TIP**

● Task 1

Practise using modal + have + past participle by completing these sentences.

a) I could have gone to the concert, _____ .

b) You might have seen me _____ .

c) She would have written to your parents _____ .

Managing shifts in your writing (including subjunctive mood)

Level 6 writers should be able to use and manage a range of verb forms accurately to help clarify and emphasise meaning.

Shifts in verb forms

Verbs have different tense forms which indicate different times:

(1) **present tense** for actions happening now

(2) **past tense** for actions that have already happened

(3) **future tense** for actions that will happen in the future.

The verb tense within a sentence or a related group of sentences should not shift without a reason.

 **TOP TIP** A shift between verb forms means to change from one tense to the other. **TOP TIP**

Sometimes shifts in tenses make perfect sense, as when you describe an event that takes place before another event:

> At the first Christmas concert the children will sing some carols that they learned during the autumn term.

Shifts in voice

Sentences can be written in the active or passive voice. The active voice is when the subject performing the action is emphasised:

> Carla made the cake.

The passive voice is when the subject performing the action is de-emphasised:

> The cake was made by Carla.

Shifts in mood

People have moods such as happy, tired, lonely and many more. Your writing has two moods: indicative and subjunctive.

 A sentence in the indicative mood is a statement of fact.

 A sentence in the subjunctive mood indicates that something is conditional or doubtful.

In the subjunctive mood:

I was → I were

It was → It were

If I were rich, I would buy a blue, sporty car.

If it were not for you, I would have no money.

It is not correct to write 'If I was …' or 'If it was …' These 'mistakes' are considered shifts in mood.

Shifts in person

There are three forms of narrative voice in writing:

1st person: I or we

2nd person: you or you (plural)

3rd person: he, she, they, etc.

Sometimes when you speak you shift the person. In writing this does not sound fluent and is rarely used. For example:

Incorrect: I used to think reading wasn't that important, but as **you** get older, **you** get a lot wiser.

Correct: I used to think reading wasn't that important, but as I get older, I am getting a lot wiser.

Task 1

Here are some phrases which can be used to create a sentence written in the subjunctive mood: *as it were, be that as it may, far be it from me, heaven forbid, if need be, so be it, suffice to say.*

Write a sentence using the following fixed expressions:

a) far be it from me _____

b) if need be _____

c) heaven forbid _____

Active and passive

Sentences can be active or passive. Therefore tenses also have active forms or passive forms.

When do you use the passive and active voice?

Normally, when the performer of the action (the agent), is made the subject of the verb, it comes first and you use the active form of the verb. The other person or thing in the sentence is the object of the verb.

The girl was chasing the dog.

subject   verb   object (the girl is doing the chasing)

A sentence is active when the subject is doing the action (verb).

However, if you want to focus on the person or thing affected by the action, you make the person or thing the subject of the sentence and use the passive voice.

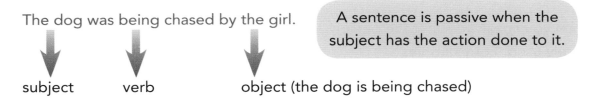

The dog was being chased by the girl.

subject   verb   object (the dog is being chased)

A sentence is passive when the subject has the action done to it.

When do you use the passive voice in preference to the active voice?

① You do not know who the agent is:	I had the feeling that I was being followed.
instead of	I had the feeling somebody was following me.
② When it is obvious to the reader or listener who the agent is:	I had been told that the shop was closed.
instead of	The manager had told me that the shop was closed.
③ When it is not important to know who the agent is:	I don't need a lift, I'm being picked up.
instead of	I don't need a lift, someone is collecting me.

Rewriting active sentences as passive, and passive sentences as active

① This sentence is written in the active form:	Some hunters in England are still killing foxes, even though the general public disagrees with fox hunting.
② The same sentence has been rewritten as a passive sentence:	Foxes are still being killed by hunters in England, even though the general public disagrees with fox hunting.

Task 1

Read the sentences below and write **A** if the sentence is written in the active form or **P** if it is written in the passive form.

a) Osian collected the rounders equipment from the yard. _____

b) Ashley blew the candles out on the cake. _____

c) The dog was fed by Bianca. _____

d) Abisha brushed El-Gibbor's hair. _____

e) The bus conductor checked the tickets. _____

f) The pencils were sharpened by Sundus. _____

Task 2

Practise writing in the active and passive forms by completing the table.

Active	Passive
Mum made the beds.	
	The classroom was tidied by the Year 6 girls.
	The winning goal was scored by the defender.
The teacher put up a display.	

Adverbs and pronouns

Adverbs modify verbs, adjectives and other adverbs. Most adverbs describe the manner (how), time (when) and the place (where).

TOP TIP Many adverbs end with -ly such as quietly, slowly, carefully. However, some adverbs do not end with -ly such as later, tomorrow, early, daily. **TOP TIP**

Task 1

Add examples of adverbs telling you manner, time and place to the table below.

Manner (how)	Time (when)	Place (where)
bravely	tomorrow	above

Pronouns

A possessive pronoun: refers to a specific person/people, thing/things belonging to a person/people (and sometimes belonging to an animal/animals or thing/things). A possessive pronoun can be the subject or the object and can refer to a singular or plural.

our cat, her sister, my ring, your house, their chairs, its tail

A personal pronoun: takes the place of specific nouns (the names of people, places and things). For example:

I, he, she, me, you, they, him, her, us, we, it

A relative pronoun: relates subordinate adjective clauses to the rest of the sentence. For example:

that, which, who, whom, whose, whichever, whoever, whomever

Expanded noun phrases

You can add detail to sentences by expanding the noun phrase or by adding an adverbial. You could add more detail before and after the noun. There are many ways to add more detail:

(**1**) adding adjectives

(**2**) adding a prepositional phrase

(**3**) adding an adverbial.

For example:

(**1**) the car

(**2**) the blue sports car

(**3**) the car near the church

(**4**) the blue sports car near the church

(**5**) the shiny blue sports car

(**6**) the car in the showroom window

(**7**) the shiny blue sports car in the showroom window

(**8**) an exquisite environmentally-friendly car behind the ambulance.

Remember to use precise language which will create vivid description for your reader. Refer to the sections about prepositional phrases, adverbials, adverbs and adjectives to recap on how you can make appropriate choices when creating expanded noun phrases.

Task 1

Add some words before and after the following nouns to create expanded noun phrases.

a) a ball _____

b) the party _____

c) a bird _____

Changing nouns to verbs and changing verbs to nouns

You will need to know how to change nouns to verbs.

Noun	Verb
confusion	to confuse
failure	to fail
delivery	to deliver
struggle	to struggle
decision	to decide
meeting	to meet

You can change verbs to nouns by adding -tion, -ism, -ness, -ist and -it.

Verb	Noun
to learn	learning
to educate	education
to style	stylist
to travel	traveller
to tour	tourist
to reduce	reduction

Task 1

Complete the following table changing nouns to verbs and verbs to nouns.

Verb	Noun
	worker
to write	
	picture
	anger
to dress	
	coward
	happy

Word families

Level 6 writers should use most words, including more difficult words, correctly.

Word families are words that can be grouped in a particular way:

(1) through a spelling pattern

(2) meaning

(3) by the inclusion of a particular root word.

Word families are important because they sometimes reveal hidden patterns in words that you already know. For example, the verb roots receive, deceive, conceive have the corresponding nouns reception, deception, conception.

Task 1

Complete the table below by adding the noun.

Example	Noun	Verb	Adjective
dedicate		dedicate	dedicated
improve		improve	improved
organise		organise	organised
behave		behave	behavioural
produce		produce	productive
inform		inform	informative
imagine		imagine	imaginative
dominate		dominate	dominant
signify		signify	significant

Task 2

Write a sentence using each of the following words.

a) dedicate _____

b) productive _____

c) dominate(d) _____

d) significance _____

Punctuation and clarity

Punctuation plays a very important grammatical role. It can also let the reader know what intonation patterns the text would have if it were spoken aloud. Here are the basic rules for the use of each punctuation mark.

Use a capital letter

(1) for all proper nouns (Dave, London)

(2) for all proper adjectives (adjectives derived from proper nouns: Italian, Shakespearian)

(3) for the first word in every sentence

(4) for races, nationalities, languages and religions

(5) for words in a title, except articles (a, an, the), short prepositions and short conjunctions (The Owl and the Pussycat)

(6) for some abbreviations.

 **TOP TIP** All of the following need capital letters: days of the week, months, holidays, holy days, events in history, political parties, official documents and trade names. **TOP TIP**

Use a full stop

(1) to end a sentence that makes a statement or gives a command

(2) after each initial in a name (J.K. Rowling)

(3) after each part of an abbreviation (p.m., B.C.) but not if the abbreviation is an acronym (NSPCC).

Use a question mark

(1) at the end of direct questions.

Use an exclamation mark

(1) to express strong feelings; it may be placed after a word, phrase or sentence.

56

Use a comma

(1) to separate individual words, phrases or clauses in a series

(2) to enclose an explanatory word or phrase inserted in a sentence (Dawn, a mother of two talented sons, won the lottery last week)

(3) to separate co-ordinating adjectives (adjectives that equally modify the same noun: The doctor sat on the smooth, soft, comfortable chair)

(4) to separate items in an address or a date or to separate the exact words of the speaker from the rest of the sentence ('Good night,' Mum said, 'sleep tight').

Use a semi-colon

(1) to join two or more independent clauses that are closely related but are not connected with a co-ordinating conjunction (I have a friend called Claire; she is a football fan).

Use a colon

(1) to introduce a list

(2) after the character who is speaking in a play-script

(3) to emphasise a word, phrase, clause or sentence that explains or adds impact to the main clause (Alan has only one thing on his mind: profit).

Inverted commas are

(1) also known as quotation marks or speech marks

(2) placed before and after direct quotations or speech ('I'm really not sure,' she said, 'whether we should go away now or in September').

Task 1

Rewrite the text below as direct speech using inverted commas accurately.

Milva asked Miss McCoy for some help with her homework. Miss McCoy suggested that she should come to booster classes on Mondays or Wednesdays.

_____

_____

_____

57

Using apostrophes, dashes and brackets accurately

Apostrophes can be used for two reasons:

For omission	For possession
This is also called contraction, where a letter or letters are missed out, for example could not is the expanded form and couldn't is the contraction.	The possessive form of singular nouns is usually made by adding an apostrophe and s (girl's). The possessive form of plural nouns ending in -s is usually made by adding just an apostrophe (teachers'), for plural nouns not ending in -s, an apostrophe and s (children's).

You may be asked to add the apostrophes to a piece of writing. Read the instructions carefully as they might tell you how many apostrophes are required.

Dashes and brackets

- indicate a slightly longer pause than a comma. This can build tension and indicate comic timing. He was on track to beat his personal best, reached the last corner of his final lap – and fell at the finish line.

- enclose an explanatory word or phrase inserted in a sentence, serving the same function as brackets (parentheses), or commas. The Taj Mahal – one of the Seven Wonders of the World – took 22 years to build.

- brackets allow the writer to speak directly to the reader in an aside: She was standing in a magical space (you know what I mean), or they may be used in stage directions for play-scripts: Greg: (*pointing at chair*) Sit down!

Task 1

Complete the table by putting a tick to show if the apostrophe is used for contraction or possession.

	Possession	Contraction		Possession	Contraction
can't			Bal's bag		
the boy's coat			the children's books		
I'm			doesn't it		

Task 2

Write a sentence using brackets and write it again using dashes.

Brackets _____

Dashes _____

Etymology

Etymology is the study of words and how they have changed over time.

Knowing where a word came from and how its meaning has changed over time may help you to learn new spellings.

Native words are words that we have inherited from the English. They were brought to England by Germanic migrants (Anglo-Saxon was also heavily influenced by the language of the Vikings). Most of our everyday words are derived from this category.

Words from Latin, which for many centuries was the only language used in scholarship, provide much of our technical and learned vocabulary (e.g. the word vocabulary). But many Latin words actually come from Greek.

Words from Greek are widespread in the areas of knowledge that were first developed by the ancient Greeks (e.g. geometry, philosophy).

Words from other languages include Arabic (algebra), Italian (spaghetti), Spanish (armada), German (kindergarten), Hindi (shampoo) and many others.

Task 1

Using a dictionary, find the definition, origin and word class for each of the following words to complete the table.

Word	Definition	Origin	Word class
pragmatic			
ubiquitous			
pretentious			
cynical			

Prefixes and suffixes

Knowing prefixes and suffixes and their meanings helps in building multi-syllabic words, especially where sounds change.

Prefixes

 Task 1

Complete the following table by adding an example word using the prefix.

Prefix	Meaning	Example word
anti- ant-	against / opposite	antibiotic
fore-	before	
inter-	between	
post-	after	
co-	together	
il-	not	
ir-	not	
mid-	in the middle of	
semi-	half	
hyper-	more than normal	
trans-	across	

Suffixes

 Task 2

Complete the following table by adding an example word using the suffix.

Prefix	Meaning	Example word
-acy	state of being	piracy
-ist	one who does	
-dom	place or state	
-ess	female	
-tion / -sion	state of being	
-ster	person	
-ness	state of being	
-ize / -ise	to make or become	
-ic / -ac	like, pertaining to	
-ous	having / full of	

Homographs and homophones

Homographs

This word comes from the Greek words homos, meaning the same, and graphein, meaning write, and means words that are spelt the same, but have different meanings and, often, different pronunciations. For example:

bow as in bow and arrow

bow as in bow down

minute as in a minute creature

minute as in wait a minute

Homophones

This word comes from the Greek words homos, meaning the same, and phone, meaning sound, and means words that are pronounced the same, but have different spellings and meanings. For example:

feet / feat

knight / night

Task 1

Complete the following table by adding a homophone for the word in the first column, or a word often confused with it, and its meaning.

night – the opposite of day	knight – a man who served his sovereign or lord as a mounted soldier in armour
Chile – a country in South America (noun)	
flour	
write – (verb)	
peace – freedom from war	
rain – (verb)	
stationary – stop, at a standstill	
sight – what you see	

Identifying syllables

As words become more complex, they don't always follow a simple spelling rule. Instead, you may find it helpful to visualise how the different syllables are spelled and then put the word back together. For example:

> horrible = hor + ri + ble

You will need to use your knowledge of suffixes when identifying the syllables -tion, -cian, -ble.

You can use your knowledge of one word to help you with similar words. For example:

> identity = i + den + ti + ty
>
> identify = i + den + ti + fy
>
> identical = i + den + ti + cal
>
> identification = i + den + ti + fi + ca + tion

Task 1

Write out the missing syllables for the following words:

a) person = _____ + _____

b) personal = _____ + _____ + _____

c) impersonal = _____ + _____ + _____ + _____

d) personality = _____ + _____ + _____ + _____ + _____

e) impersonate = _____ + _____ + _____ + _____

f) personify = _____ + _____ + _____ + _____

g) personification = _____ + _____ + _____ + _____ + _____

+ _____

ANSWERS

(The answers below are examples of Level 6 responses.)

Identifying points in a text (page 7)

1. Anthony Horowitz uses a letter as the opening to his book, which is an appealing way to engage with the reader – the reader and writer immediately have a relationship whereby the writer entrusts the reader with sensitive information by confessing to a recent violent experience.

2. The author originally refers to the streets as being 'pretty mean'. However, the author quickly extends his description by underlining the word 'mean' to emphasise just how mean they are. By juxtaposing 'pretty' and 'mean', the author develops his description by denying that the streets are pretty.

Using information from different sources (page 9)

1. Subjective: *China Road* (extract 1): any evidence which is opinion such as: 'There is nothing quite like it', 'You can keep Fifth Avenue', 'This is my favourite, it is all here', 'China may be on the edge of greatness again'. Objective: *The Rough Guide to China* (extract 2): any factual evidence such as: 'Huangpu River', 'Pudong, 1949', 'Zhongshan Lu, Wai Tan' (literally 'outside beach').

Using quotations (page 11)

1. 'The most seductive thing in the world.'

2. 'It is a thing to change your life.' (*The language in this question clearly states that copying a short quotation such as this one is enough to merit a mark.*)

3. You get the impression that Behala and the children who live there are very poor because of the description, 'The Behala children are beautiful and to see them on the rubbish tips all day can break your heart'. Using such powerful language stresses that the conditions for the children in Behala must be bad. The author also states that working in Behala makes you feel like 'you're making a difference'. He shares his personal viewpoint to stress how tough it is for these people.

Different meanings (page 13)

1. Using the clues from this text readers may come to the conclusion that the characters are about to jump from a plane using a parachute ('leap of faith') or are preparing to enter a mine or water ('checking our safety equipment', 'lowered myself deeper and deeper').

2. This answer involves more thought from the reader as the author does not explicitly state how the character is feeling. Instead the reader needs to find clues which hint at how the author is feeling. In this paragraph we sense that the character is about to embark on a real challenge ('leap of faith'). The main character is feeling apprehensive about the forthcoming experience ('Today

was tough … tougher than I could ever have imagined') and is unsure if Dave, his usually reliable colleague, will support him ('eyes were covered'). The main character is also excited / worried about lowering himself deeper as his 'heart beat like a drum'.

3. To emphasise that the author has made decisions in life before but this is by far the toughest. This is also exaggerated by the title of the extract.

Organisation of the text (pages 16–17)

1. The opening section immediately addresses the reader by stating, 'If you're reading this book …' The author continues to involve the reader throughout this section ('If you're a normal kid …', 'But if you recognise …') which strengthens the writer / reader relationship. The author also uses a short sentence, 'Read on'. The effect of choosing to command the reader with two simple words is almost perceived like an order would be.

2. Rick Riordan teases us, the readers, at the end of this extract, almost daring us not to read any more and choosing to end the introduction with a 'don't blame me' attitude. The title of the chapter would also appeal to young people who would share the excitement of accidentally vaporising their teachers!

3. The character clearly does not want to be a half-blood. The author chooses to make this the first piece of information he shares with the reader. The author then stresses the dangers of being a half-blood.

Themes and purposes (page 19)

1. a) The writer presents the title, **Four Leopards Killed Weekly in India**, in bold to separate it from the rest of the news article. The abbreviations **WWF** and **TRAFFIC** are also in bold as they are the names of charity organisations and are explained in the text. b) Quotations increase authenticity and evoke emotion. c) To strengthen the article and to prove the point being made.

Explaining how language is used (page 21)

1. Alliteration: chuckling children; torturous teachers. Personification: the chairs stood at attention for inspection, the pencil seemed to scream 'use me!'

Language choice and effectiveness (page 23)

1. When you need a knife, you find 10,000 spoons; one minute you meet the man of your dreams and the next you meet his beautiful wife; death row pardon two minutes too late; dying the day after you win the lottery.

The effect of sentence structure (page 25)

1. To evoke humour and show the fun Smudger and Leroy are having. These words are outlining Leroy's thought process too.

2. To demonstrate Leroy's reluctance to answer Smudger. Each time Leroy repeats this trio of words, the reader anticipates what his answer will be.

Writers' techniques (page 26)

1. make us laugh, frighten us, teach us a moral, question our beliefs, make us sad, shock us, tease us, manipulate us

Commenting on a writer's viewpoint (page 28)

1. suspense / scared / cautious; using ellipses / repetition / incomplete sentences

2. The extract starts with a rhetorical question to engage the reader and persuade them that they should buy the book. Using 'if so,' reels the reader in; the writer is almost throwing the bait and letting the reader snatch it. 'Purchase me today' is a personal plea by the book; it makes the book speak for itself. The reward for the buyer will be getting on 'the path to sucess'.

Understanding a writer's point of view (page 29)

1. a) The boy isn't daft because he is one step ahead of the teacher and other children. He has the last laugh as he wins in the end. b) The teacher has been set a target which is unrealistic and the teacher can't achieve it as the boy has made up a nonsense word for the teacher to spell which is ironic as the whole poem is about the boy not being able to spell.

2. 'Gust Becos I Cud Not Spel' is a poem which demonstrates how children who struggle with their spelling are set up to fail in our school system. It states that 'boys in school... some of them laffed' and 'some of the girls... who laffed a lot'. However, the main character has taken revenge and turned the tables around, flipping conventional society on its head. For the character is now in charge: 'I am the dictater' and all those who ridiculed him / her are being punished, especially the teacher who will never succeed with his challenge, as the main character has made up a nonsense word the teacher will never be able to spell.

Language and the effect of time (page 31)

1. hot: attractive, handsome; tight: mean with money; burn: transferring data using technology; sweet: something that is awesome or great

ANSWERS

2. Modern readers may interpret 'wicked' to mean cool, brilliant or attractive, whereas more traditional readers would understand it to mean that Osian was evil, mean or a bad person.

Texts from different times and places (pages 32–33)

1. tick: good overcomes bad; a character learns a lesson

2. a) Dates back to at least eighteenth century, refers to common practice in the sixteenth century, where blackbirds would escape from cooked pies. b) First published in 1830, inspired by a real incident where a girl, Mary Sawyer, brought her pet lamb to school. c) One theory is the destruction of London Bridge by Olaf II of Norway in 1014. d) Makes reference to the Great Plague in London during 1665.

3. Both poems cover **similar** themes such as identity and belonging. The writer of 'Island Man' longs to return to his homeland and dreams of the sound of the sea waking him 'to the sound of the blue surf'. **Similarly**, the writer of 'The Fringe of the Sea' reflects on waking to the sound of the sea too: 'We do not like to awaken Far from the fringe of the sea.' **However, the poems do vary** as in reality the writer of 'Island Man' is actually in London and dreaming of his home, **whereas** the author of 'The Fringe of the Sea' lives close to the sea.

Cultural and spiritual influences (page 34)

1. The language in this extract suggests that the setting is America during the time of the Civil War and at the end of slavery ('Christmas of seventy-six') and the writer refers to the 'Northern soldiers', 'Southern whites' and 'free Negroes'. Other references imply that life was very hard for black people – 'as hard being free as it was being a slave'. This character's speech is written in the dialect spoken by black Americans at the time: 'And the colored folks … was, well, we was just tired.'

Introduction to writing (page 35)

1. This is an opportunity for pupils to identify their strengths and areas for development. It is a self-assessment and they should choose phrases from the table. There is no right or wrong answer.

Informal and formal language (page 36)

1. Informal: Hey / Hi / Hello – accept abbreviations: Hey Ma8; Cheers / C U later; Formal: Dear / To whom it may concern; Yours sincerely / Yours faithfully

Imaginative vocabulary and language (page 37)

1. light / slow / cold / ugly / quiet / happy / big

2. red: crimson, scarlet, cardinal, cherry, ruby, brick, vermillion; yellow: gold, lemon, saffron, maize, champagne, citrine, topaz

Parts of speech (pages 38–39)

1. a) an / the, a / the, some / the, a
b) an, an, some, the

2. a) shouted / screamed / yelled b) sprinted / raced

3. a) haven't you? b) won't I? c) couldn't she?

Nouns (page 41)

1. Proper nouns: Edinburgh, Lisbon, Washington, Judy, Amir; Common nouns: elephant, person, parrot, desk, dinner; Collective nouns: armada of ships; atlas of maps; brace of grouse; buffoonery of orangutans; Abstract nouns: sadness, health, hatred, illness

Connectives and cohesion (page 42)

1. Achieving a Level 6 in writing is not an easy feat. To begin with, you will need to control your viewpoint and write accurate and well punctuated sentences. You may need some revision materials to support you such as Rising Stars books! However, you will also need to read a range of good quality texts too. Overall, you will need to challenge yourself and prepare for some hard work.

Identifying phrases (pages 44–45)

1. a) SNP: the ninety-year-old man / the top goal-scorer b) ONP: the crooked path / the golden boot award

2. The teenagers in Manchester dressed in 1970s fancy dress outfits and danced through the streets to raise money for their local charity.

Identifying independent and dependent clauses (page 46)

1. a) She went to bed early because she was tired. She went, because she was tired, to bed early. b) He tried to do his best in school whenever he could. Whenever he could, he tried to do his best in school.

Tenses and modal verbs (page 47)

1. a) if I had enough money. b) if you had been there earlier. c) if she was in a bad mood!

Managing shifts in your writing (including subjunctive mood) (page 49)

1. a) Far be it from me to complain, but it is rather cold in here. b) I will come back after the meeting if need be. c) I hope it doesn't happen – heaven forbid.

Active and passive (page 51)

1. a) A b) A c) P d) A e) A f) P

2. The beds were made by Mum. The Year 6 girls tidied the classroom. The defender scored the winning goal. The display was put up by the teacher.

Adverbs and pronouns (page 52)

1. Manner: accidentally, fast, hard, carefully, straight; Time: tonight, daily, regularly, monthly, normally; Place: behind, there, far, here, elsewhere

Expanded noun phrases (page 53)

1. a) the shiny, round, red cricket ball on the ground b) the fun birthday party at Ella's house c) a big blue bird sitting on the tree

Changing nouns to verbs and changing verbs to nouns (page 54)

1. to work / writing / to picture / to be angry / dress / to be cowardly / to be happy

Word families (page 55)

1. dedication; improvement; organisation; behaviour; production; information; imagination; dominance; significance

2. a) I dedicate this award to my parents who have always encouraged me to do my very best. b) We worked well today – all in all, it has been a productive afternoon. c) The champions dominated the second half and managed to retain their lead at the top of the table. d) What is the significance of this data?

Punctuation and clarity (page 57)

1. 'Can I have some help with my homework, Miss McCoy?' asked Milva.

'You could come to booster classes on Monday or Wednesdays if you want,' suggested Miss McCoy.

Using apostrophes, dashes and brackets accurately (page 58)

1. contraction, possession, contraction, possession, possession, contraction

2. Shelly won the race (despite having hurt her arm) by a huge distance. Shelly won the race – despite having hurt her arm – by a huge distance.

Etymology (page 59)

1. pragmatic: relating to matters of fact or practical affairs / Latin word for skilled in law / adjective; ubiquitous: existing or being everywhere / first known in 1830 / adjective; pretentious: attempt to impress by affecting greater importance / from 'prétentieux' in French / adjective; cynical: distrustful of human nature / first known in 1542 / adverb

Prefixes and suffixes (page 60)

1. foreword; interwoven, post-mortem; cooperate; illegal; irresponsible; midpoint; semicircle; hyperactive; translate

2. pianist; kingdom; actress; extension; gangster; happiness; maximise; aquatic; delicious

Homographs and homophones (page 61)

1. chilli – food (noun); flower – plant (noun); right – opposite to left; piece – part of something; reign – to rule (verb); stationery – writing material; site – location

Identifying syllables (page 62)

1. a) per + son b) per + son + al c) im + per + son + al d) per + son + al + i + ty e) im + per + son + ate f) per + son + i + fy g) per + son + if + ic + a + tion